Perfect Praise

I0187140

Accurate Praise & Worship that actually gives God pleasure!

Rudi Louw

Copyright © 2014 by Rudi Louw Publishing

All rights reserved solely by the author. No part of this book may be reproduced in any form *without the permission of the author.*

Most Scripture quotations are taken from the *Revised Standard Version*, Holy Bible, Thomas Nelson Publishers. Copyright © 1983 by Thomas Nelson, Inc.

Some Scripture quotations were taken from the *New King James Version*, Holy Bible, Thomas Nelson Publishers. Copyright © 1983 by Thomas Nelson, Inc.

All Scripture quotations not taken from the RSV, or NKJV are a literal translation of the Scriptures.

The Holy Scriptures are just that, HOLY.

Statements enclosed in brackets were inserted into Scripture quotations to add emphasis or clarify the meaning of what is being said in those scriptures. The integrity of God's Word to man was not compromised in any way. Due care and diligence was cautiously exercised to keep the Word of Truth intact.

For example: The apostle Paul said in his second letter to Timothy in chapter three verse sixteen that:

"All Scripture is given by inspiration of God (literally God breathed)*, and is profitable for doctrine, for reproof, for correction, for instruction **in righteousness**,"* NKJV

Content

The marvel of the Holy Bible

1. The *theme* and *inspired thought* of Scripture continues *uninterrupted*.

It took *1,500 years* to compile the Holy Bible, involving *more than 40 different authors*, yet the theme and inspired thought of Scripture continues *uninterrupted*, from author to author, from beginning till end.

2. *Absence* of mythical stories:

Compare philosophies and theories about creation in the Middle East, Europe, Asia, Africa and Latin America, and you'll find mythical scenarios, gods feuding and cutting up other gods to form the heavens and the earth. In ancient Greek mythology, the Greeks see Atlas carrying the Earth on his shoulders. In India, Hindus believe 8 elephants carry the Earth on their backs.

But in contrast, Job, the oldest book in the Holy Bible, declares that *God suspends the earth 'on nothing.'* (Job 26:7)

This was said millennia before Isaac Newton discovered the invisible laws of gravity that delicately balance every planet and sun in its individual circuit.

In contrast to every other ancient attempt to give a creation account, *the Holy Bible pictures the creation of the Earth in a very scientific manner.*

In Gen 1 for instance, the continents are lifted from the seas, then vegetation is formed and later, animal life, all reproducing *'according to its own kind,'* ***thus recognising the fixed genetic laws.***

Finally we have the bringing forth of man and woman, *all done by God in a dignified and proper manner, without mythological adornments.*

The rest of the Holy Bible follows suit.

The narratives are ***true historical documents,*** *faithfully reflecting society and culture,* ***as history and archaeology would discover them thousands of years later. Not only is the Holy Bible historically accurate, it is also reliable when it deals with scientific subjects.***

It was not written as a textbook on history, science, mathematics or medicine, *yet, when its writers touch on these subjects, **they often state facts that scientific advancement would not reveal or even consider until thousands of years later.***

While many have doubted the accuracy of the Holy Bible, time and continued research have consistently demonstrated that the Word of God is better informed than its critics.

3. The Holy Bible is *intact*.

Of all the ancient works of substantial size, *the Holy Bible against all odds and expectations survives intact.*

Compared with other ancient writings, the Holy Bible has more manuscripts as evidence to support it than any ten pieces of classical literature combined!

The plays of William Shakespeare, for instance, were written about four hundred years ago, and written after the invention of the printing press. Many of his original words have been lost in numerous sections, *yet the Holy Bible's uncanny preservation has weathered thousands of years of wars, contradictions, persecutions, fires and invasions.*

*Jewish scribes, **like no other manuscript has ever been preserved**, preserved the Holy Bible's Old Covenant text through centuries. **They kept tabs on every letter, syllable, word and paragraph**.*

*They continued from generation to generation to appoint and train special classes of men within their culture **whose sole duty it was to preserve and transmit these documents <u>with perfect accuracy and fidelity</u>**.*

Who ever bothered to count the letters, syllables, or words of Plato, Aristotle or Seneca for that matter?

When it comes to the New Testament, the actual number of preserved manuscripts is so great that it becomes overwhelming.

There are more than 5,680 Greek manuscripts, more than 10,000 Latin Vulgate manuscripts and at least 9,300 other versions; there exist a further 25,000 manuscript copies of portions of the New Testament.

No other document of antiquity even begins to approach such numbers.

The closest in comparison is Homer's <u>Iliad</u> with only 643 manuscripts. The first complete work of Homer only dates back to the 13th century.

4. In dealing with time, the Holy Bible *accurately foretells what will happen ahead of time, with unmatched results.*

No other ancient work even begins to attempt this.

Other books claim divine inspiration, such as the Koran, the Book of Mormon, and parts of the Veda.

But none of these books contains predictive foretelling.

This one fact we know for certain, and it is undeniable: *While microscopic scrutiny would show up the imperfections, blemishes and defects of any work of man, <u>it magnifies the beauties and perfection of God</u>, just as every flower displays in accurate detail, the reflection and perfection of beauty, <u>so does the Word of Truth when it is scrutinized</u>.*

Historian, Philip Schaff wrote:

'...Without money and weapons, Jesus the Christ conquered more millions, than Alexander, Caesar, Mohammed and Napoleon.

Without science and learning, He (Jesus the Christ) shed more light on things human and divine than all philosophers and scholars combined.

Without the eloquence of schools, He (Jesus the Christ) spoke such words of life as was never spoken before or since and produced effects, which lie beyond the reach of orator or poet.

Without writing a single line, He (Jesus the Christ) set more pens in motion, and furnished themes for more sermons, orations, discussions, learned volumes, works of art, and songs of praise, **than the whole army of great men of ancient and modern times combined.***'* (The person of Christ, p33. 1913)

Today, there are literally billions of Bibles in more than 2,000 languages,

...*isn't it about time you find out what it really has to say?*

Hey listen, the Holy Bible is all about Jesus, the Messiah, the Christ,

...*and everything about Jesus Christ is really about YOU!!*

Study Tips:

Read 2Corinthians 5:14, 16, 18, 19, and 21.

In the light of these Scriptures it should be obvious that if you want to study the Holy Bible,

…you should study it in the light of mankind's Redemption!

Daily feed on Redemption Realities, found in the book of Acts, Romans 1 through 8, Ephesians, Colossians, Galatians, 1Peter 1, 2Peter 1, James 1, 1 and 2Corinthians.

Acknowledgement

I want to acknowledge and thank one of my mentors in the faith, Francois du Toit, for blessing and impacting my life with revelation knowledge.

The portion on *"The marvel of the Holy Bible"* was borrowed from his website: http://www.mirrorword.net/ as students so often feel they have a right to do with things that come from teachers they respect. Just as Galatians 6:6 says: *"Let him who is taught the Word **share in all good things** with him who teaches."*

To all our dear friends and family, and to those who helped me with this project,

…but especially to my wife Carmen,

For all the love and support,

THANK YOU!

Foreword

Thank you for taking the time to read this book.

Let me start off by saying that *I am totally addicted to my Daddy's love for me;*

…I am in love with Jesus Christ, *and that is enough for me!*

The love of God is so much more than a doctrine, a philosophy, or a theory; it is so much more and goes so much deeper than knowledge; *it way surpasses knowledge,*

…we are talking heart language here,

…therefore this book was not written to impress intellectuals with knowledge and philosophy, theologians with theories and doctrine, nor English majors with grammar and spelling for that matter,

…so if you come up with any other definitions or find any language inaccuracies, please don't use it to disqualify Love's own message I bring to you in this book.

I write *to impact people's hearts;*

…to make them see the mysteries that has been hidden in Father God's heart, concerning

Christ Jesus, and really *concerning THEM,* so as to arrest their conscience with it, *that I may introduce them to their original design, and to their true selves;* **and present them to themselves perfect in Christ Jesus,**

...and set them apart unto Him ***in love,*** as a chaste virgin,

We are involved with the biggest romance of the ages;

...therefore this book cannot be read as you would a novel; *casually.* It is not a cleverly devised little myth or fable.

It contains revelation and *truth* into some things you may or may not have considered before. It is not blasphemy or error though.

It is the TRUTH of God, ultimate TRUTH, and therefore has direct bearing upon YOUR life, **the Word and the Spirit is my witness *to the reality of these things!***

Be like the people of Berea the apostle Paul ministered to in Acts 17:11. Open yourself up to study the revelation contained in this book, *to see if these things are* ***true and real.***

...but be forewarned, do not become guilty of the sins of the Pharisees, ***or you too will miss out on the depth of fulfillment God Himself, who is LOVE, wants to give you.***

(Jesus said of the Pharisees and Sadducees that they strain out every little gnat BUT swallow whole camels. What He meant by that is that *some people seem to have it all together when it comes to doctrine and they love to argue.*

It makes them feel important, but it is nothing other than EMPTY religious and intellectual pride.

*They know the Scriptures in and out, and YET they are still so IGNORANT about **REAL TRUTH that is only found in LOVE;***

…they are still so ignorant and indifferent **towards the things that REALLY MATTERS.**

They are always arguing over the use of *every little jot and tittle* and over the meaning and interpretation of *every word of Scripture.*

The exact thing they accuse everyone else of doing though; the precise thing they judge everyone else for, *they are actually doing themselves,* that is: **they often completely misinterpret and twist what is being said, making a big deal of insignificant things,**

…while obscuring or weakening God's real truth; the truth of His LOVE

They are always majoring on minors, **<u>because they do not understand the heart of God</u>**

...and therefore they constantly miss the whole point of the message.)

Paul himself said it so beautifully:

*"...the letter kills but **the Spirit BRINGS LIFE;"***

*"...knowledge puffs up, but **LOVE EDIFIES."***

I say again:

Allow yourself to get caught up in the revelation I am about to share.

Open yourself up to study the insight contained in this book *not only with a desire to gain knowledge, but also with anticipation **to hear from Father God yourself;***

*...**to encounter Him through His Word;***

*...**and to embrace truth, in order to know and believe the LOVE God has for <u>you</u>,***

*...so that you may get so caught up in it, **that you too may receive from Him; LOVES' impartation of LIFE***

*If you take heed to these things, and yield yourself fully to it, **it is custom designed and guaranteed to forever alter and enrich your life!***

"…I pray that
your contribution,
meaning,
your participation
and sharing together
in the faith
may become effective,
and promote **only**
the knowledge of Him,
meaning
the grace of God,
what He accomplish
and communicates
in His grace, in His work of
redemption

to you, and also
to the rest of mankind

"...I desire that
as you acknowledge
these things only
in your fellowship together,
that your fellowship,
your KOINONIA,
**your active acknowledgement
of God's truth,
and your sharing
of God's faith
together,**
and your celebrating

together
in these things,
in other words
**your praise and worship
together,
may not be hit and miss,
but become affective!"**

"That means
it will have a big impact
on yourselves
and others
**as you are together
promoting only
the knowledge**

of every good thing
that is ours
in Christ Jesus,"

"Meaning
you are exclusively promoting
every good thing
that is in us,"

"...that is **already** in you"

"...in your identification
of your eternal union
with Christ Jesus!"
                    - Philemon 1:6

Prayer

Father we thank you *for what You've given to us.*

We thank you *for Your precious Word.*

We thank you *for one another.*

We thank you *that we may see in one another* **the very same value that You see in us.**

We thank you Father that *as we begin to appreciate Your estimation and opinion; Your favor and measure of our lives,* **our opinion of one another increases.**

Thank you that today *we may regard and value one another and make room for one another's input* as we meet together in fellowship Lord;

…we may honor, we may treasure one another as we recognize the work of grace in each other.

Thank you Lord!

We praise you Lord!

We thank you *for the Holy Spirit.*

We thank you that *as we open the Scriptures, that He comes to teach us and reveal to us the wealth of knowledge hidden in language, hidden in words, the language of the Scriptures,*

…***and that this knowledge becomes our sustenance***

In Jesus Name, *let it be just so!*

We praise you Father!

Amen!

Chapter 1

Fellowship beyond temporal values and temporal realities

You know, God **does** exist and you can do only one of two things with God, *you can either praise Him or you can ignore Him.*

You can either praise Him *or ignore Him.*

But you can't make Him disappear and go away!

He is *more real* than anything!

*He is the author of **reality**!*

He is reality Himself!

Praise is not something we do on a Sunday morning *only.*

And talking about Sunday mornings, or whatever day we decide to meet, *our meeting shouldn't just be a gathering together for a religious service either.*

It should really be **a celebration.**

**That celebration we enjoy in our meetings
is really just a culmination of our gathering
together during the week, spontaneously,
for fellowship in one another's homes and
in the marketplace.**

So our celebration meeting is just *a gathering,
a culmination of our fellowship,*

...a gathering where we come together *to just
give voice and volume to our appreciation of
His provision,* **of what He has given us in His
grace.**

In my teaching in this book, *I want us just to
concentrate* **on our appreciation of His
provision in His grace; in His work of
redemption.**

It is so wonderful to know that the foundation of
our fellowship *is more than just some kind of
religious definition that we seek to identify
ourselves with,*

...*it is more than just coming to a place on a
specific day, to meet in a specific building,*

...it is more than just speaking a particular
dialect of Christianese, you know, *our own
specific doctrines and particular religious
philosophy,*

...***it is even more than just speaking the
language of righteousness,***

*...but our fellowship, the foundation of our fellowship, **is founded upon something that God initiated.***

Would you go with me to the book of Philemon in your Bible, and we are going to concentrate on verse 6.

This might be the first time you've ever turned to this page in your Bible, but it's the little book just before Hebrews.

Philemon 1:6

"...and I'm praying that <u>the sharing of your faith</u> <u>may promote the knowledge of all the good things that is ours</u> in Christ Jesus."

So, when Paul speaks to the Church here, He says in another translation,

*"I desire **that your fellowship...**"*

(*"Koinonia"* is the Greek word he used here for the word, *"sharing"*)

In other words, he says:

*"... I desire **that your participation; your sharing together, your fellowship, your Koinonia <u>will promote the knowledge</u>...**"*

The New King James Version says:
*"...**will <u>acknowledge</u> ...<u>every good thing that is in you</u> in Christ Jesus**"*

27

In Romans chapter 1, we see how **God did not leave Himself without witness.**

God gave enough witness of His Deity, of His omnipotence, of His greatness in creation, *so that man in his senses may make contact,*

…so that man may begin to appreciate the fact that there is an intelligent Originator of all that is manifest in this physical realm;

*…so that man **may begin to appreciate** that there is an intelligent origination, **an intelligent reason,***

*…**a desire in the heart of God that is the origin of it all.***

But Paul says that created man **fails to acknowledge God,**

*…**even though the knowledge of God is apparent,***

*…*man failed to acknowledge Him *and we began to ignore the Creator*

…and began to just limit our appreciation of life to what the senses could appreciate of the natural.

And so here in Philemon Paul says that *he desires that our fellowship will extend beyond a mere appreciation of **temporal values, and temporal realities,***

…but it will be *a communication of every good thing that is ours,*

…*every good thing that is in us in Christ Jesus,*

God through Paul desires that our fellowship together will be,

…*the acknowledgement of all that is ours in Christ,*

…*of all that is revealed in Christ concerning man*

And we want that **to be our focus,**

…*so that our celebration is rooted and sustained,*

…*in the revelation,*

…*of all that God has in mind for man*

Chapter 2

The accurate appreciation of God

Do you see that if we want to just praise God religiously, *we will soon exhaust comparison?*

If we want to praise something or someone of beauty, *we have to begin with some form of comparison.*

I then am compelled to say:

'God, you are more precious than silver, you are more costly...'

...and somehow *I'm grasping for,*

...and trying to *gather some value that I could compare with my appreciation of God,*

...so I can at least say:

'God you're more valuable, more costly than gold, you're more beautiful than diamonds,'

*'...**than anything that I could desire**,'*

'...than anything that I could appreciate in life,'

'...than anything that makes life attractive,'

'...God you exceed that!'

And so, this inevitably leads us to study the question of **perfect praise.**

You see, **when is my praise of God perfect?**

When is my praise of God *more than a religious attempt,*

...to somehow esteem **an unknown, invisible** *being?*

Listen, my praise is only perfect,

...when my praise is *the product of His opinion,*

...of His appreciation of my life!

You see, every other standard *by which I would attempt to evaluate God,*

...would be far inferior to the God I am praising.

The word praise literally means **TO PRICE.**

So, if I want to *"PRICE"* God and say:

'God, **you are more awesome** than creation itself,

…**you are more awesome** than the universe,

…the vastness of the expanse of the universe **cannot measure your greatness**,'

…then I would still find myself inferior in my expression **to justly attribute God,**

…**to perfectly pronounce Him,**

…and **I would seek to gather even more accurate ingredients for comparison.**

I would say,

'God you're more precious **than the best experience I could ever have,**'

'…**than the greatest emotion** I could ever calculate'

'…**God you're beyond that!**'

Designed inside the heart of man is a cry,

…**to correctly appreciate the Creator,**

Designed inside the heart of every person,

…there's a desire to capture in their praise **an accurate definition** of the God who is behind their existence and their very being,

*…He is **the reason** for **their very existence.***

And so in essence Paul makes a statement in Philemon verse 6 *…a* rather bold radical statement,

He says that,

*…the **only <u>just</u>,***

*…the **only <u>perfect</u> foundation,***

*…the **only perfect <u>measure</u>** of praise,*

…of appreciation,

…of 'PRICE,'

*…***the only <u>perfect</u> praise**,

*…**is the very appreciation that God Himself reveals through His Word, of man!***

Do you see that *I cannot compare and match* **God** *with a mountain, or a tree, or gold, or silver,*

*…**and give Him <u>perfect</u> praise!***

Do you see that?

I could detect praise *through esteeming that which man appreciates **in terms of value,***

*…*and then I can say, *'God you're beyond <u>that</u>!'*

...but it won't be <u>perfect praise</u>.

It's when I tap in, *to the initiative of God* that I tap into an inexhaustible measure of revelation,

...an <u>inexhaustible measure of praise</u>.

You see faith's value does not lie in man's definition of his need.

Faith's value lies *in the revelation of God's provision.*

Now if God's provision can be *measured,*

...if God's provision can be *calculated,*

...*then faith <u>has a measure</u>,*

...but that faith does not begin with man's need,

Faith begins with the heart of God,

...with the largeness of God's compassion,

...with the largeness of His yearning,

...with the intensity of His desire, to communicate Himself, His very person, His heart, His inner-Self to man!

So, faith's origin *is the heart of God.*

What is faith's *substance?*

What gives faith *substance?*

**It is what God reveals in His Word,
*concerning Himself.***

**And God's revelation of Himself *is never
independent of His plan; of His design for
man.***

*So Paul is saying that <u>perfect praise</u> is
found <u>in the appreciation of God</u>,*

...of who He is, <u>in relationship to us</u>!

If perfect faith is found in the faith of God,

*...then perfect praise is found in the praise
of God.*

*...*perfect *'PRICE'* is found in the *'PRICE'* of
God.

*...*perfect value is found *in what God
values.*

*...*perfect approval is found *in the approval
of God.*

*...*perfect love is found *in the love of God.*

**You see every other measure of love and of
approval and of praise and of value and of
price would be imperfect.**

Because, if my measure of love is found *in my appreciation of your performance,*

...and if there is inconsistency in your performance, *then my love for you will be marred,*

...it will be imperfect!

So, if I want to perfectly love,

...if love is to be perfected,

...love must have a substance,

...love would have to have an ingredient,

...that goes _beyond_ ...the possibility of another's failure ...and short-falling,

Because you see, if my love for you is measured *by your ability to succeed,*

...or by your ability to fail,

...then my love will be imperfect,

But if I can draw from a source,

...a resource,

...that carries more integrity <u>than anything that has worth in this world</u>,

...then love is perfected.

So, praise is perfected *in the appreciation of <u>what God values</u>,*

...in the appreciation of <u>God's initiative</u>,

...in the appreciation of <u>what God believes</u>,

...in the appreciation of <u>what God believed was revealed and accomplished</u>,

...of <u>what God believed happened in the death of His Son</u>, on man's behalf, and to man!

Romans 1:16-17

16 *"...for I am not ashamed to preach the Gospel of Jesus Christ..."*

I love what the original text of that phrase *"the Gospel"* brings out.

The words in the original Greek are **EU ANGELION,**

The word **EU** actually means: **well done**.

You see it's not just *good news;*

...it's not just a good message,

*...it's a "**well done**" message. Amen!*

Hallelujah!

It's about what God already did,

...*what He already accomplished,*

...*what He brought to pass,*

...*what He brought to completion in Christ.*

You see from before the foundation of the earth already, *the lamb was as good as slain.*

God's **well done** is behind the Gospel.

And so Paul says that,

Romans 1:16-17

"...I am not ashamed of the Gospel"

(I don't need to make some apology for the Gospel),

"...for it's the power of God unto salvation..."

What measures **salvation?**

That perfect release *that man now enjoys,*

...to perfectly find and discover the definition of his life, because of Christ!

Man discovers that *grace gives new definition to my life!*

I am no longer what my job-description allows me to be.

I'm no longer what my mother hoped for me,

...*hoped I could become,*

...but I am what <u>*God*</u> *says I am.*

And *grace; the work of redemption, gives me that definition.*

Hallelujah!

And so, *when I discover in the mirror of the Word, my true identity,*

...*there's an immediate embrace in my spirit, in my inner man, of this Gospel,*

...*of the very power of God,*

...*unto salvation,*

...releasing me from anything that would hold me captive, *to anything less than,* what <u>God</u> sees in me, and for me!

Listen, the effect of the Gospel is measurable, it's called: *perfect faith!*

The effect of the Gospel is not measured in, you know, *whether you smoked,* **but now you've stopped smoking,**

…and whether you drank, *and now you've stopped drinking alcohol,*

…and whether you were living in adultery, *and now you've stopped your sinning.*

That's not the measure of the Gospel!

The true measure of the Gospel is, *Man finding again true value,*

…Man finding again the place of perfect fulfillment,

…when he discovers again his original design in Jesus, the Master Copy,

…when he discovers himself in the mirror of Christ!

Beholding Him, *as in a mirror,*

…seeing what He reveals,

…seeing yourself, your original design, your true identity, your true self by God's design, seeing that version of you, in Him,

…seeing you in Him, that is the true measure of the Gospel!

Hallelujah!

That is what the effect of the Gospel is measured by!

You see, the Law and religious legalistic do's and don'ts could get you to stop drinking,

…the Law could get you to start behaving better,

…*but it'll never fulfill you.*

The problem with the law of works *is that it never permanently satisfies the flesh.*

God wants total fulfillment for you!

And to get you into that place of total fulfillment, *He wants to draw you into acknowledging everything good that is already within you,*

…*as it was and is revealed in Christ Jesus.*

Hallelujah!

We are still in Romans,

Paul says,

Romans 1:16,

"…*I am not ashamed of the Gospel of Jesus Christ,*

…*it's the very power of God unto salvation…"*

Verse 17 says,

"...for in it (in this Gospel, in this *"well done"* announcement)

...the righteousness of God is revealed (it has become apparent),

...from faith to faith..."

God wants us to discover that our standing before God, *our righteousness;*

...my approach before the Father <u>is the product of the faith of God</u>

God calls the things that are not as though they are.

Because in Him *they <u>are</u> reality!*

And if He says they are, *then they <u>are</u>!*

It's reality!

...ready to manifest!

God began to anticipate man's total restored standing before Him,

...and so His faith made that provision!

His faith made it *a reality!*

And *that provision,*

…that reality <u>revealed</u>,

…is the measure of our praise!

That provision and reality <u>revealed</u>,

…gives substance to our appreciation of God!

Chapter 3

Our value and worth to God

Turn with me to Hebrews chapter 2.

I want to read to you from verse 6, but I first want to bring your attention to the fact that verse 6 is a direct quotation from Psalm 8.

So I am going to just read to you Psalm 8, but we will get back to Hebrews 2:6.

Psalm 8:1-9

*"**O Lord our Lord, how majestic Your name is in all the earth. You whose glory above the heavens is chanted!***

*…by the mouth of babes and infants **You have perfected praise**."*

The New King James Translation says,

*"Out of the mouth of babes and infants **You have ordained strength,** because of Your enemies, that You may silence the enemy and the avenger"*

Verse 3 says,

"When I look at Your heavens,

...the marvelous work of Your fingers,

...the moon and the stars,

...which You have ordained and established,

...what is man (in comparison with all that) that You are mindful (mind-full) of him..."

Can you see how man's appreciation of God, was restricted and reduced, **because of the Fall** *that was introduced by the fall of Adam?*

Man's appreciation of God,

...his appreciation of himself, **of his make-up, of his design, of God's handiwork in him** was now **reduced.**

Man's appreciation of God was now reduced to *a mere comparison between the creation, the stars, the moon,* **the external.**

Because, within himself, *he had to live with the results; the effects of the Fall.*

...he had to live with that condemnation and that sense of inferiority:

'What is man, I mean, how can man compare or compete with the vastness of the universe?'

'You see, we are so ugly, man is so ugly,

…man is such a sinner and a looser,

…how can there possibly be a comparison between man and God?'

Psalms 8:3-6

"When I look at Your heavens, the marvelous work of Your fingers, the moon and the stars, which You have ordained and established,

…what is man that You are mindful (mind-full) of him?"

…that You make so much of him?

…that You care for him?

…that You bother to visit,

…that You bother to give attention to,

…that You bother to actually constantly take care of him?

David goes back to the beginning of creation *and makes a discovery that answers his question* and so he says in verse 5,

"…BUT, You have made him a little less than God Himself, and thus You have crowned him with glory and honor"

*"**You have given him dominion** over the works of your hands;*

*...**You have put all things under his feet!***"

Now back to Hebrews chapter 2,

Hebrews 2:8

*"**You have given him dominion** over the works of Your hands;*

*...**You have put all things under his feet!***"

...and in 'putting everything in subjection under his feet,'

*...**He left nothing outside his control!***"

...as it is, we do not yet see everything in subjection under him,'

(He is quoting man's reasoning *under the influence of condemnation and a sense of inferiority,*

...but he is about to answer them back)

Verse 9,

*...**BUT** we see Jesus,*

...who for a little while was also made lower than the angels,

...nevertheless, He was crowned with glory and honor,

...because of the suffering of death, (or to endure the suffering of death)*,*

...so that, by the grace of God,

...He might taste death <u>for everyone</u>."

Another translation says:

"...and He, for a little while was made lower than the angels, <u>but we see Him crowned with glory, and with honor,</u>

...and through the suffering of death, and <u>by the grace of God</u>, He tasted death <u>for everyone</u>."

Verse 10,

"For <u>it was fitting</u> for Him,

...for whom and by whom all things exist,

...<u>in bringing many sons back into glory</u>,

...that He should make the Pioneer of <u>their</u> salvation <u>perfect</u> through His suffering"

(Note: Jesus was the perfect Pioneer, **His pioneer work, not Jesus, but His work, <u>our salvation</u> was <u>perfected</u> [it was successfully accomplished], through His suffering**.)

"For He who sanctifies (through His suffering)

...and those who are being sanctified (through His suffering)

...have all one origin,

...that is why He is not ashamed,

...to call them His brethren (His family)*,"*

...saying: 'I will declare Your name to my brethren;

...In the midst of (as part of) *the congregation,*

...I will sing praise to You (...or *praise will be perfected*)*.'*

What do we see when we see Jesus?

Jesus spells out in capital letters:

MAN'S VALUE & MAN'S REDEMPTION!

Do you see if my praise limits me to a sentimental appreciation of a man who lived a wonderful life, and died a sad death, but then was raised and went back to His Father, now over 2014 years ago,

...then my praise will fail to appropriately and perfectly appreciate God?

What I am saying is that I can only praise God _perfectly_,

...I can only begin to _accurately_ and _successfully_ praise God,

...by _comprehending_ man's value to God as demonstrated in the work of redemption,

...by beginning to measure,

...and correctly evaluate and 'PRICE' and treasure _the purpose of God with man_,

..._as it is revealed in Jesus_!

You see we've read verse 8,

...and oh, how we love to get stuck in verse 8 and say,

'Well ...'**As it is we do not yet see everything in subjection under our feet'**

But hey, listen, when God created man,

...He **_"crowned man with glory and honor,"_**

...and obviously when God _"**crowned man**"_

...it wasn't because God just wanted to decorate man,

...so man could just look nice, you know, for the opening ceremony you know,

No,

Obviously God desires to extend in that *"crown" His own dominion.*

God saw in man *the full representation of Himself,*

...He saw in man *the very representative that He Himself qualifies* **to represent His dominion** **upon the earth.**

God *"crowned"* **him,** *with His own opinion,*

...with honor!

God *'PRICED'* **man,**

God *valued man!*

He values man, *with His own preciousness,*

...with the exact design, *which God carried in His own bosom;*

...within Himself,

...within His own makeup,

...within the makeup of His very own being,

...for all eternity!

But now it says,

Hebrews 2:8

8 …'**But as it is we do not see everything**…"

And so we've built that wonderful *theology,*

…that weird and wonderful *theory,*

…**that convenient deception,**

…around **the legal and the vital,**

…you know, **the positional and the experiential,**

…and they say, *the theologians would say,*

'*Well, it's wonderful to understand that* **legally man stands already reconciled to God,**

…**but as it is, we do not see everything in subjection to man, practically,**'

'…**we see man,**

…**still not ruling from that** "**crown**," *as you say, brother Rudi,*'

'…*but instead we see man* **being ruled by circumstances.**'

And so we have limited our experience **to what we see** in man …**and we keep adjusting our experience to that!**

We've said,

*'Well, you know, **it's impossible** for man **to really** now **live** in a practical way, the absolute success that God had in mind for him.'*

We've said,

*'It's **not quite possible** for man **to really rule**.'*

But God wants us to take the limits off of Him!

*...**to take the limits off of <u>our praise</u>!***

*...**to take the limits off of our estimation of our own worth and value!***

*...**so that we may finally rule and reign,***

*...**and be that absolute success,***

*...**and be that absolute perfect praise** God **had in mind from the beginning!***

How is your interpretation of the success of that cross?

Or rather, *forget about your interpretation!*

...forget about the interpretation of man!

Let me ask you this:

How do we see the interpretation _there in that Scripture_ of the success of the cross?

The writer of Hebrews *interprets it for us;*

He left no room for us to come up with our own interpretation of Psalms 8:6

He interprets it there for us in Hebrews 2:8,

He says,

"...In 'putting everything in subjection under his feet,'

...He left nothing outside his control!"

Let me paraphrase that.

He is saying,

"Now that phrase, 'putting everything in subjection under his feet,'

...actually means that,

...He left nothing outside man's control!"

Did you get that?

God left nothing outside of man's control!

The writer of Hebrews is really asking *a rhetorical question.*

That means *he is not looking for the answer,*

...he already knows the correct answer,

...and now he is going to provide us with the correct answer,

...he is not going to leave a blank space open so we could fill in our own answer.

He is saying,

"...In 'putting everything in subjection under his feet,'

...did He leave anything outside his control?"

In other words,

...did God have in mind that man would actually reign with such authority that man would be the absolute king in this life?

...king over circumstances?

AND THE ANSWER IS: <u>YES!</u>

How then do we tap in?

...how do we then <u>*correctly appreciate and appropriate*</u> this standard of teaching which has been delivered to us ...this standard of <u>excellence</u> that God has in mind for man?

The very next verse says it;

...it gives us the answer,

Hebrews 2:9

9 *"__BUT__ we see Jesus..."*

I want to suggest to you that *how you see Jesus makes all the difference in the world!*

It is how you see Jesus that makes the difference!

When you see Jesus as *the* one success out of 5 billion, *__then God's a failure__.*

If Jesus was the only success, the only one that did it, *then after 5 billion tries, then God, You must be a failure!*

What do you see in Jesus?

I see in Jesus *the __Pioneer__ of __my__ SALVATION!*

...__my__ salvation!

I see Him as doing __exactly__ *that which will release the human race*,

...from the dominion of everything that belittles man,

I see Him as doing <u>exactly that</u> which will release the human race *from that <u>which reduces man to less than</u> what God always had in mind for man.*

I see Jesus <u>successfully pioneer</u> *man's release!*

...*man's escape from the dominion of sin!*

...so that I'm no longer looking at Jesus as an excuse for my own failure,

...but I'm looking at Jesus *as the release from my sins!*

Sometimes you know, we decide to go out to eat a hamburger somewhere,

...let's say it's at Mc Donald's, or Burger King, or Wendy's, or whatever your fancy is,

...and by the time you get there you can already taste that juicy hamburger they have on display there on that menu board,

...you know they make those pictures look so good,

...it's all there man, I mean, it's bursting at the seams; *it's the best looking hamburgers you've ever seen,*

...but then you know, when you receive your order, *it's not quite, you know, **the same,***

...it doesn't measure up.

And so what you do is, you eat, *and you just ignore what's in front of you,*

...and you just keep looking at the picture you know,

Ha...ha...ha...

...and while you're looking at the picture, you think to yourself,

*'Oh man, this is... yeah... man it's just better this way, just looking at the picture... yeah... at least, you know, when I taste **I can just make believe** it's the same thing,*

*...because I paid some good money, you know, and I don't want to throw this poor excuse of a burger away, **so now I'll just have to eat it**, whether I like it or not!'*

Now that's deception,

...that's deceiving yourself!

...and God is not about to deceive Himself, amen!

Listen, **God is not interested in *alternative fulfillment!***

God is not about to use deception *as an alternative to His fulfillment!*

He is not about to deceive Himself!

...and rob Himself of His own fulfillment!

Man is the object of God's desire!

And so God's not going to deceive Himself,

...by just, you know, *looking at the picture, looking at the perfect, looking at Jesus,*

...and then *just putting up with an inferior you!*

It's how we see Jesus <u>*that releases us*</u>*!*

How we see Jesus *releases us ...into the full appropriation* of what He successfully achieved!

...and therefore also into the full appreciation <u>of what He sees in us</u>!

...<u>and appreciates about us</u>!

Hebrews 2:9

"<u>BUT</u> we see Jesus ...<u>crowned</u> with glory and honor..."

We see Him,

Verse 14,

"...partaking of flesh and blood."

We see Him,

"...who sanctifies,

...and those who are sanctified in His redemption,

...as ALL having one origin," verse 11 says.

...as coming from the same factory, from the same kitchen, amen!

Hallelujah!

God is not trying to, kind of, you know, *paint a picture that is too good to be true.*

'You see it's wonderful, you know, brother Rudi, it's wonderful that God anticipates all this for man,'

'...but as it is...'

'...I mean, just read the newspapers man!'

"BUT we see Jesus..."

You see if I see Jesus *independent of what He reveals about man and achieved on man's behalf,*

...then my praise will be made imperfect!

...then my fellowship will be made imperfect!

...my very fellowship with Him *in the spirit,*

...will be made imperfect!

...as well as my fellowship with my brothers and sisters!

...and with my fellow man!

Because *I've seen my brother,*

...and the suspicion in my heart will soon be justified,

...that my brother is not quite there yet,

...and immediately the disappointment will begin to rule me.

And you know what I'll do?

...instead of celebrate him,

...instead of praise him,

...instead of valuing him,

I'll ignore him.

And you know whom I'm really ignoring?

God!

That means *I will **praise,***

...***someone else's failure,***

...**and I will *elevate,***

...***someone else's failure,***

...**<u>*above the success of Jesus*</u>!**

I will put *more confidence and faith* in my brother's ability to fall,

...**than I'm putting confidence and faith in God's ability *to perfect in Christ Jesus, in that work of redemption,* for all eternity, those who draw near to Him by faith.**

Do you see what I am saying?

Do you see the difference?

The moment that *the appreciation of God,*

(...**and I've said earlier that *our praise,***

...**is the product <u>of God's appreciation of us</u>**),

...the moment that *the appreciation of God,* **enters my heart, and becomes my appreciation,**

...***then I am fully released to love with God's love!***

You see, if my love is the product *of His love for me,*

...then my praise is the product *of His praise of me, amen!*

Hallelujah!

I love Him, *because He first loved me!*

I praise Him, *because He first praised me!*

I price Him, I value Him, *because He first priced and valued me!*

When did He love me?

While I was yet hostile *in my mind!*

My *thinking* was in hostility and enmity against God and His plan,

...against His pre-ordination; *His design for me,*

...*but His love conquered me!*

And so we find the measure of our praise,

...*in the powerful revelation,*

...*of His appreciation of us!*

You see our praise of Him, is now fueled, by the initiative of God!

Chapter 4

Jesus is the mirror in which we see our true design and worth

Hebrews 2:9

*"**But we see Jesus,***

*...**the pioneer of our salvation**"* - verse 10

Listen don't see Jesus *through religious glasses.*

The world, the religious world, the Christian religious world, for centuries, *got stuck in the mud* **through their sentimental appreciation of Jesus.**

Listen to me now, *Jesus, as a man,*

...has no value whatsoever,

...*outside of what He came to accomplish!*

If the life He lived,

...if the death He died,

...if His resurrection,

...*does not confirm man's value and man's salvation,*

...*then Jesus is of no value to man!*

You can create any Jesus you like,

...any Messiah you like,

...and, o, we have seen so many different ones *just in Sunday-School alone!*

You can create any Jesus you like,

...any Savior you like,

...as a Jewish man told me just a few days ago,

'My hero is my coming Messiah,

...because he gave me this more brilliant job opportunity.'

You see you can create any Messiah you like,

...any Savior you like,

...*but if Jesus is not what God spelled out to the world,*

...*then it's not the real Jesus.*

Jesus once asked His own disciples,

"Who do men say that I am?"

…not that their opinion will change His identity!

He wasn't asking them to guess,

…to come up with their own philosophy and conclusion,

No,

He wanted to see *if they knew the truth,*

…if they would *come to the right mathematical conclusion,*

…the right conclusion about Him,

…the truth about Him!

You see man would add his guess and add his philosophy,

…and add his doctrine and his definition,

…but what the Father reveals of Jesus,

…that is the only real identity of Jesus.

And when the Father revealed Jesus to man, *He did not reveal a super human.*

Let me say that again,

When the Father revealed Jesus to man, *He does not reveal some historic, super human,*

...He reveals a man as he always had in mind for man to be!

He reveals <u>you</u> in His Son, amen!

Have you not read Hebrews One?

Let's just quickly take a look at Hebrews 1.

He says,

Hebrews 1:1

*"**In many and various ways** (in incomplete pictures and fragments of thought) **God spoke of old, to our forefathers, by the prophets, <u>but</u> in these last days He has spoken to us by His Son.**"*

*"**He has spoken a final word to us that is the beginning and end-all of everything!**"*

*"...**He has spoken SON to us** (...and in us)"*

Now, you'll remember Colossians 3, where it says,

Colossians 3:16

*"**Let the Word of Christ dwell in you, richly...**"*

And sometimes we think,

'Well, if I can just know a 155 Bible verses, then the Word is dwelling in me richly.'

'...If I could, you know, quote Moses up and down, and inside out, then, you know, the Word dwells in me richly.'

'...If I can quote the 10 commandment verbatim, or if I can tell you the books of the Bible, in order, you know, then the Word...'

Listen, the richness of the indwelling Word is directly related to *the measure of the revelation alive in your heart, of the word of Christ.*

What is the Word of Christ?

It is the Gospel!

It is what God spoke to man in Christ!

You see when God spoke *He had an audience in mind*.

When you write,

...you know, *that inspired love letter,*

Ha... ha... ha...

...you have an audience in mind.

I mean, **she might not even know that you exist,**

…but there you are, **_anticipating her response,_**

…and you're reading that love letter to yourself, you know, _before you're going to send the thing off,_

…and you're reading it again, and again, and again,

…**_and you begin to live in the anticipation of her response._**

You have an audience in mind!

…and you have feedback in mind,

…and communication and mutual appreciation,

…and everything that goes with fellowship, or "Koinonia" (…intimate relationship).

You have an audience in mind!

And when God speaks _He's not wasting words!_

God is saying something _to this human race!_

He spoke in fragments through the prophets,

...just wetting men's appetite,

...to again appreciate *a place of innocence,*

...a place of quality intimacy with God!

God spoke through the Law,

...and He spoke through the prophets,

...in fragments,

...to awaken in man again, that jealous anticipation, of standing fully clothed in God's approval again.

But then God SPOKE in Jesus,

...no longer in fragments!

...no longer in riddles!

He spoke a WORD so clear,

...it can no longer be mistaken!

...or ignored!

He spoke *a final word,*

...in Jesus!

...in the incarnation!

...in the work of redemption!

71

I said earlier that,

...it's the richness of the indwelling Word of Christ,

...it's that richness,

...that insight and revelation,

...that fuels your faith!

...that fuels your praise!

...that fuels your love!

...that fuels your total expression in your Christian walk!

Hebrews 1:2-3

"...God spoke in these last days by His Son, whom He appointed heir of all things, through whom also He created the world,

*...Jesus reflects **the glory** of God"*

The New King James Translation says about Him, in verse 3,

*"...who being **the brightness** of His glory and **the express image** of His person..."*

In Colossians 1:15, it says,

*"...He **makes visible** the invisible God"*

72

The word: *"**glory**"* speaks of *a measure,*

*…it speaks of **an opinion**.*

So, *"He reflects **the opinion** of God…"*

He displays ***exactly*** *the opinion of God,*

*…**the exact opinion,***

*…**the accurate measure,** of God,*

*…**the accurate measure,***

*…**of both man and God!***

On one of my recent trips to Africa I was sharing with one of my spiritual sons,

…we were talking one day about this exact spiritual truth, and we just had a camera film developed, and I said to him,

'you know, if one of these pictures would be spoiled, say for instance coffee is spilled on it or something, and the image is spoiled,

*…**as long as we have the negative,***

*…**as long as the negative is preserved,***

*…**we still have that same image captured, the same colors, the exact same image remains captured in the negative.***

*...and so, in spite of Adam's transgression, **in spite of man's Fall,***

*...**God captured, forever, in His Son,***

*...**all that He had in mind in His original design of the human being!***

Our original value is captured and preserved,

*...**and then revealed and restored there in Him, in Jesus!***

*...**Our true value, amen!***

Isn't that wonderful!

Hallelujah!

And through the gospel,

*...**through that word of faith,***

*...**God now again births again His exact image,***

*...**His exact likeness,***

*...**in the heart of faith!***

Amen!

Hallelujah!

Hebrews 1:3

"He reflects the glory (the opinion) of God and bears the very stamp of His nature..."

In Philippians 2:8, it says that,

*"He was found in **fashion** like unto a man"*

The word *"**fashion**"* in the Greek speaks of,

...***the external form,***

...and you know, ***that really blesses me!***

Because it means that, *even though Jesus submitted His Deity, His being, His person, to an external physical form, **to a human body,***

*...**it did not in any measure reduce the quality of His person; the quality of His nature!***

That human body did not give Him any excuse to live a life of less excellence than what He always lived before!

Because it says in Colossians 2:9 that,

*"...**In Him** (in Jesus) **all the fullness of God dwells bodily** (**in a human body**)..."*

So, God's not saying,

'Well for 33 years, you know, Deity will have to kind of, you know, **lower its standard a little bit,**

...because of the flesh; because of the human body,

...so, let's just use the body as our justification, as a good excuse for sin.'

No!

He displayed, *in this earthen vessel*,

...*in this human body we claim to be <u>our problem</u>,*

...*our excuse*,

...He displayed *in this earthen vessel*,

...*all* of Deity,

...*all* God-likeness,

...*all* godliness,

...*all of it!*

What was the purpose of God behind this display?

Was it just to somehow brag with what He's always had ...*and so,* **to ridicule us some more,**

…and say,

'See what miserable failures you are compared to Me!

…you can and will <u>never</u> measure up!'

No!

It was to awaken man again!

When man sees Him,

…he sees the mirror of his own identity!

Hebrews 2:9

"But we see Jesus…"

You see **if I look at <u>man</u>,** *I see failure,*

…but I've looked at <u>Jesus</u>,

…and looking at Jesus <u>*I see into a mirror,*</u>

…I see, the success of *what I am!*

…looking at Jesus, *I see that I'm a success!*

Hebrews 1:3

"He reflects the glory **(the opinion)** *of God and bears the very stamp of His nature …<u>upholding the universe by His word of power</u>…"*

What is God's, *"word of power?"*

It's His love for us!

It's our value to Him!

It's YOUR SALVATION!

Do you see that?

We get so religious when we read our Bibles; when we read the scriptures,

...and, 'Brother we've got to be word people!'

...and so we read the word; we read the Scriptures,

But, brother, sister, **what is THE WORD?**

THE WORD is that which God so clearly spelled out <u>in His Son</u>, *concerning you!*

Do you know that the whole universe *is* upheld by God's opinion of you!

...by His love for you!

Can you now see how futile it would be *to seek to praise God perfectly* **by comparing Him with the universe!**

...while missing His plan of redemption!

...misinterpreting it!

O, religion really gets carried away in thinking about, and speaking about, and singing about, this mystic Being *beyond their reach!*

"Great is the Lord, and greatly to be praised!"

"Oh, the Lord is so magnificent!"

…and they all agree, and say a loud amen to that!

…but, begin to measure God for His plan of redemption,

…and suddenly man stands embarrassed,

…religion stands embarrassed,

…it cannot measure that!

…they cannot measure that, not accurately,

…so with the very same voice that they esteem and praise this great and marvelous, mystic God,

…they insult Him!

…they insult Him in the way they interpret and measure and appropriate,

…the redemption of Jesus Christ!

The only accurate measure of our praise, *the only perfect measure,*

...is the way we first measure and understand,

...and then how we embrace and appropriate redemption!

...it's how we appropriate redemption!

...that's the only accurate measure of our praise,

...it's the only perfect praise we can possibly give Him,

...appreciating and appropriating redemption accurately,

...and completely!

The accurate and full appreciation and appropriation of God's plan of redemption is the only quality that gives praise substance!

...otherwise you are missing it in your praise!

...otherwise your praise is just another guess!

...yet another guess that misses the mark of what you and God could be!

Salvation cannot be over exaggerated; *it can only be under estimated!*

'If things could just be the way God always had in mind,

…and if I could just be the way God always had in mind, **then it could be like this**

…and maybe I could be like that…'

…and I just add all the attributes that I would like God to be like, and that I would like myself to be like…

Listen, God displayed Himself in man,

…He displayed Himself in a man, in His Son!

In John 12 the Greeks came, and they wanted to see Jesus.

And the disciples thought,

'Wow, this is our opportunity, you know,

…Jesus, You can get even more popular today, boy oh boy, this is going to be great!

…because the Greeks have come all this way to see You,

…and if we can just begin to line up all the sick and get Jesus to heal them and do all those mighty miracles,

...then the Greeks are going to go home, impressed! '

...but you know the Bible says that,

"Jesus went and hid Himself from them!"

Why?

...because He already said:

"The hour has come for the son of man to be glorified!

...for the kernel of wheat to fall into the earth and die,

...and produce a harvest, beyond the limits of just one seed,

...after its own kind!"

You see God only has **one kind** in mind;

...God doesn't have various kinds in mind!

'Let's be broad in our doctrine, brother,

...to accommodate, you know, man's clumsy efforts,

...and man's clumsy definitions of Deity'

Listen man, God only has *one kind* in mind,

   ...and it's the kind that He is the origin of!

...the kind that He carries the master copy of!

...the only kind that will satisfy His heart!

...not through an empty guess,

...and a high falutin empty address,

...but because He has created a design that would satisfy Him!

It satisfies Him!

Do you think a manufacturer could enter into his holiday, and into his rest, before his product is perfected or until his product is perfected?

It's not likely to happen!

You see, the very rest, the very Sabbath that God has entered into, *guarantees the perfection, the completion, of His creation!*

Hallelujah!

The boundary lines have fallen for me in pleasant places!

You are my worship, *and I am yours!*

As I find my fulfillment in encountering Him, *so He finds His fulfillment in encountering me!*

Religion ...Christianity itself, *has no value, outside of this reality!*

Religion ...Christianity, **will always be caught up in works,** *no matter how accurate those works are in accordance with Scripture,*

...as long as those works add to me,

...and add to who I am before God,

...as long as those works add weight and faith to my conduct,

...it will rob me of the intimacy I have been designed to enjoy!

O, I can memorize and quote my little Scriptures, and read the Bible, and do my morning devotions and say my prayers and do my religious thing, **but I am unfulfilled!**

...I remain unfulfilled!

God jealously yearns for your spirit!

...because He knows your design!

I met and visited with a Christian business man from Atlanta a little while ago now, and we have been friends for a while. But lately he has been struggling to keep the business afloat, *and he is depressed,*

...and yet he is very involved in practicing all the strong scriptural business principles,

...I mean, he even teaches it in the big church he is a part of.

After a long conversation with him, I couldn't help it anymore, I grabbed him by the arm and looked him in the eyes, and I said to him,

'I set you free in Jesus name!'

I found myself very compelled to say to him,

'Brother, let me tell you something very vital for you to understand:

...the measure of your success is not your business, it's not how many scriptural principles you can relate to your business,

...but the measure of true success is the intimacy that you and I enjoy with the Father!*'*

You see, we can get so distracted,

...believing God for greater and greater projects, for big success,

...but we are missing out on the truth of our design!

You see, if you want to start appreciating His provision,

...there is only one way you can do it,

...it is through appreciating and appropriating what His provision equals you and so equips you to enjoy!

And you see, *appropriating His provision is not,*

...appreciating what faith <u>can give me</u>!

...but appreciating what faith <u>has given me</u>!

The faith of God has given me the approval of God!

...that faith of God, established me in Christ Jesus,

...so that I may now have unhindered, unlimited approach before Him,

...and enjoy Him without interruption!

That's what faith has given us.

That faith quality is the only ingredient that pleases God!

God cannot be pleased, *because He cannot be fooled, <u>by anything else</u> ...by any alternative that religion has to offer!*

God has His *own kind* in mind, amen,

…and it is His own kind, His own seed, His own incorruptible seed,

…that is producing His own harvest, in your life!

Hallelujah!

"…but we see Jesus!"

I mean, what is man?

Let's go and ask our fellow man what his opinion is of man?

'O, man's just a failure, like the rest of us!'

But let's ask *God!*

God has only one opinion of man!

…and He displays His opinion, for all eternity, in His Son!

God is not about to adjust His opinion to man's failure!

Because in His Son, *the failure of man was dealt with!* Did you know that!

Listen, He was wounded for our transgressions.

He was bruised for man's failure!

The punishment that was man's due, was upon Him,

...so that the wrath of God against Sin could be perfectly satisfied in His Son's obedience!

...to perfectly release mankind!

We are still reading in Hebrews 1:3,

He says,

"...upholding the universe by His word of power..."

The whole universe is being upheld by the word of His power.

It's the same word that God spoke to us in His Son!

It's not speaking about a different word here.

Listen the whole universe exists because of one specific purpose only:

It exists because of God's heartbeat of eternal companionship with man!

The invisible cause of gravity and distance and form and fashion exists for one purpose only:

Jesus displays the plan of God with man.

The universe has no other definition, or reason for existence!

...no other definition!

...no other reason for being, for existing!

Love was and is both the cause of it and the reason for it being upheld!

The universe would fail otherwise!

And it will fail one day and no longer be needed,

...not because God will fail in His love, and finally give up on man,

...but because, **mankind as a whole will finally realize and fulfill the desire and plan in the heart of his Maker!**

Hebrews 1:3 goes on, and it says,

"When He had made purification for our sins, He sat down at the right hand of the Majesty on High,

...having become as much superior to the angels, as the name (as the identity and as the reputation) *that He has obtained, is more excellent* (more praise worthy) *than theirs,"*

Verse 5,

"For to which of the angels did God ever say, 'You are My Son, today I have begotten You!'?"

Can you see how that identity of Jesus,

...*our identity revealed in Him*,

...*is the source of our appreciation towards God,*

...*the source of our praise of Him!*

That appreciation, that enjoyment and living the life of that identity *is the best praise we can give Him!*

It is what perfect praise is all about!

That successful work of our redemption is where perfect praise stem from!

...*that's where our genuine appreciation and genuine praise of Him stem from!*

If that doesn't put a song in your heart I don't know what will!

...*that's what true praise and worship is all about!*

Let me tell you, this truth; what is revealed in redemption, *will bring about a new language,*

...even in our current Spirit filled Praise and Worship!

That new language of Grace;

...that new language of redemption,

...coming forth,

...through revelation truth; through insight and revelation,

...it is transforming and will continue to transform, even our Praise and Worship songs!

The songs we sing today will have to change; *we will not be able to sing them anymore,*

...because the spirit of wisdom and revelation in the knowledge of Him, the Holy Spirit Himself, *will not allow us to sing them anymore,*

...because they do not line up with God's truth ...with New Testament realities ...with Redemption Truth,

...with our original design and true identity revealed and restored to us in Jesus!

The Holy Spirit, the spirit of wisdom and revelation in the knowledge of Him, *will not allow us to sing those songs anymore,*

...because they do not line up with God's opinion of us revealed and put on display in Jesus!

...and because they do not line up with God's own revelation of Himself in His Son!

Only an accurate appreciation and full embrace of redemption realities, *through revelation, through faith's insight,*

*...*will produce perfect praise!

Accurate praise, perfect praise, is only the fruit, the end result of an accurate appreciation and full embrace of redemption realities!

And in that environment, *the imperfect is done away with!*

*...*whatever remains that is still imperfect; inaccurate, *no matter how much we like the song,* gets challenged to the core and is soon to be discarded as worthless, unsatisfying!

I am telling you, there is a revolution and a total transformation coming in the Praise and Worship songs we sing, *and it is here already!*

Chapter 5

The testimony of God is much greater!

Go with me to Hebrews 12.

Hebrews 12 begins with a, *"Therefore."*

And that, *"Therefore"* refers to what God reveals in Hebrews 11 on faith.

It says, *"Now faith is the substance of things hoped for…"*

Now what gives it the substance?

What gives it the substance to my hope?

You see, *"Faith is now the substance of things hoped for,"* so, what was the hope of man?

Jesus Christ is the desire of the nations!

Why?

Because man has a hope, he has a dream inside him that drives him to the next experience.

Hope believes that, *'If I can have such-and-such a vibe, then I can be fulfilled!'*

'…man, if I can only have that vibe, then I'll be fulfilled!'

What was and is the substance of man's hope?

To discover again, *the design of his nature!*

To discover again, *approval and friendship with God!*

Verse 2 of Hebrews 11 says,

"By faith, men of old received Divine approval."

The word, *"approval"* there in the Greek means, ***"testimony."***

"By faith, they received testimony."

Now 1John 5:9 says,

*"We have received the testimony of man, **but the testimony of God is much greater!"***

You see man's ability to approve of you is limited to the impression …the good, or the bad impression that you are able to make upon them.

But the approval of God is related to only one testimony: *His Son Jesus Christ, and what God saw in His Son.*

You see *God* wrote that living epistle, *He* wrote that living letter, *He* wrote the content of that letter!

You see *He understands what it says!*

He understands what is said in His Son!

He understands the testimony of His Son!

...the testimony His Son bore of us, of our design, and of our innocence and restoration now in His work of redemption!

I remember in school how we had to study poetry you know, we have to try and ascertain, and decipher, what was in the mind of the author of this poem.

...and if you don't know much about poetry, man, you can just go and interpret anything out of that thing!

Ha... ha... ha...

It's like trying to interpret some person's painting nowadays!

Ha...ha... ha...

But if you tap into the heart of the Father,

...then you can actually accurately understand what He says!

God really has only one thing in mind, *and it is man!*

I am telling you, *He is head over heels in love with you!*

God is like a young man, beside himself, *He just can't get you out of His mind!*

He has engraved you upon His heart; *upon His own consciousness!*

You know the strongest bond in human relationship exists *between a mother and her suckling child!*

There is no stronger bond in any human relationship than *between a mother and her babe that she breast feeds and nurses!*

And Isaiah says that **even they may forget their suckling child,**

"But I will never forget you!"

"...I have engraved you upon the palms of My hands!"

That means that God's relationship towards you, is stronger that even a mother's relationship with here precious little baby!

God says,

"My bond with you is stronger that father-son, stronger than husband-wife, stronger even than mother-suckling babe,

...because you are eternally Mine, you are My portion forever, I have engraved you not only upon the palms of My hands,

...see My hands, see My feet, see My side!

...but even more than that,

...I have engraved you upon My very being, I have engraved you into My inner consciousness, into My spirit, into My own heart!"

Listen, God has given Himself to you *beyond the point of no return,*

...in more ways than one!

...in every possible way, amen!

Back to Hebrews 12, so, Divine testimony, Divine approval was and is the substance of man's hope!

It's what motivated man in his religious approach!

But now, *faith,* has given substance to this hope!

"Therefore,"

Hebrews 12:1,

"Therefore we now fellowship and share the testimony of the men of old who walked in Divine approval!"

"...who walked in an understanding of God's appreciation of them!"

What was the promise of Abraham?

Righteousness, *by faith,*

...that man would again be accounted, the friend of God!

It says there,

Hebrews 12:1,

"Therefore, since we are surrounded by so great a cloud of witnesses,"

What is that cloud?

What makes up that cloud?

It is God's testimony,

...seen by and spoken of by all these other men, who prophetically pointed, towards <u>my</u> redemption!

The writer of Hebrews says,

*"…let **us also**, lay aside every weight and sin which clings so closely, and let **us** run with perseverance the race (or the task of believing) that is set before **us**."*

…and just to come back to Hebrews chapter 2 verse 8, *"…as it is, we do not yet see everything subject to man"*

…and now man gets all cluttered up and confused in his mind, because,

'Oh I know I'm supposed to be a success, but I'm a failure. I'm supposed to be happy, but I am miserable. I'm supposed to love everybody, but I hate this one, and I resent that one. I'm supposed to be, because the Bible does say that I am, but you know in technical living terms, where the rubber meets the road, it just doesn't work for me you know.'

Listen, the Bibles says,

"Therefore, since we have this faith, and since we have such a great cloud of witnesses, lay aside…"

Now how do we lay aside that weight?

How do you lay aside the failure of yesterday, and that sin which is so close at hand?

Let's read on, *because He is about to tell us how.*

Hebrews 12:2,

"Looking away <u>unto Jesus</u>, the author and finisher of our faith!"

"Therefore, if any man is in Christ, he is a new creation, the old things have passed away..."

When and where did they pass away?

In Christ Jesus, in His death on that cross, they passed away.

They passed away in God's records!

Listen, in the mind of God, *the old things do not exist!*

...anything with its hold on you *that is not consistent with the design of man,*

...*God has purged and obliterated from His memory,*

...*and thus He also stripped it of its power!*

And now notice, that scripture in 2Corinthians 5:17, does not say,

*"...**behold the old** that has passed away."*

No!

It says,

*"...**behold the new that has come!**"*

Behold the new, amen!

So, the only way you can rid yourself of the old is, *by beholding the new,*

*...**by beholding Him!***

Hebrews 2:8,

"...O, we do not see everything subject to man,"

Verse 9,

"But we see Him..."

*"...**we see Jesus!**"*

Hebrews 12:2,

*"**Looking away <u>unto Jesus</u>**..."*

...and how do we see Jesus?

'O, He was a wonderful man, who lived a marvelous life and died a sad death and then went home to be with God His Father up in heaven'

'...and what if He was, and what if he did ...so what?'

No, listen, *we see <u>Him</u>*...

"...*<u>the author and finisher of my faith</u>*"

...and what is my faith now?

"...*the substance of things hoped for!*"

What I've always hoped to be, *I found in Christ!*

I found in Him the me I've always wanted to be, the friend I've always wanted, the father I've always longed for, the mother I've never had, the companion I always knew would be mine one day!

He is the unseen *evidence,*

...*the very <u>reality</u> of things not seen,*

...*things which can only be known through faith,*

...*by embracing truth from God's perspective, from God's point of view, according to God's testimony and opinion!*

...things which cannot be seen with the mere natural eye, *with a mere natural perspective; in seeing life from a mere natural man's point of view!*

"*Looking away <u>unto Jesus</u>...*"

'O, no brother, you can't do that, **that's irresponsible!**'

Hey, no, listen, *it's the most responsible thing you can do!*

Agreeing with God, embracing His testimony of you, is the most responsible thing you can do!

It's the most responsible thing you can ever do!

*…because when you "***Look away <u>unto Jesus</u>…***"*

*…**you stop praising the problem!***

*…**and you stop being unfulfilled!***

'O, brother, let me tell you about my problem you see. O, that old devil trapped me again, and tripped me again. And let me just quickly tell you how unique I am, Satan has such a special hold on me, and he has been granted such a special privilege in my life, you know, like in Job's situation …the devil has such a special privilege in my life, he has done this and he has done that, all to test me you see, and to somehow now **improve me** you see, and he is now trying to do this, and he is trying to do that…'

Nonsense man! *That is nothing but ignorance and arrogance!*

You ain't all that and a slice of cheese!

Stop lying against the truth of redemption and the truth of who you really are in Christ Jesus!

Listen, *stop selling yourself short!*

You are totally underestimating the work of redemption and belittling it!

You are giving way to much credit to the devil!

He is a defeated foe!

Look away <u>unto Jesus</u>!

If you want to find food for your spirit,

...food that will strengthen and empower and sustain you,

If you want to find food for your praise,

...if you want to find a notion that will not be exhausted,

...so you can accurately exalt and praise God and lift Him up where He belongs,

...above my circumstance, much more powerful than my enemy, much more powerful than that thing that comes against me!

...if you want to find food for your praise,

...if you want to find a perspective and a faith that will not be exhausted,

...that will not fail you...

O, how often we want to praise God, and...

'O, God, You are so majestic, O, God You are so wonderful, and O, God, You are so great, and You are this and You are that...'

...and I learn so many wonderful King James words and Biblical terms to try and add to my vocabulary,

...and to try and extend my praise and prolong my praise and my time in His presence and to say, O, God, please...

...I will eventually get exhaust,

...and I will soon be bored praising Him!

But Hebrews 13:15 says,

"Let us therefore continually offer the sacrifice of praise..."

What sacrifice is that?

What kind of praise is that?

What kind of effort and struggle and sacrifice is that now?

I'm already exhausted and at wits end as it is!

I mean, what do I bring You, God, that will actually please You?

Listen, it's simple, it's not that complicated, **it's simply just acknowledging the name of Jesus; the work of Jesus.**

'O, but that just sounds so religious, just saying, Jesus, Jesus, Jesus all the time for hours on end.'

Listen brother, it's not that!

It is letting the word of Christ, redemption truth, redemption realities *dwell in you richly!*

It is when you begin to <u>acknowledge</u> *what God saw in His Son on your behalf that your praise finds a new volume,*

...a new resource that it may tap into!

Faith is not getting all caught up and involved in the future;

...*faith is just revealing what happened in God's heart!*

Let me say again,

...faith is not getting all caught up in end time eschatology,

...trying to see what is going to happen somewhere off in the future, or even tomorrow for that matter,

...Faith is simply getting caught up in God's heart!

...in what is revealed there!

God doesn't have a past, *He is the, I AM!*

He just expresses Himself in our time,

...so that our faith can now have that ground,

...a solid foundation that does not disappoint us!

Hallelujah!

Stop putting your faith out for, you know, for the next miracle in your life, and for the next thing, and the next thing, and the next thing...

'O, God, I am just going to get all these finance scriptures together and I'm just going to put them out there, and keep quoting them and confessing them over myself!'

Brother, no, man, that's works, plain and simple!

...and it will disappoint you again!

Don't waste your energy on those kind of spooky hit-and-miss principles.

Rather, spend your time encountering God with your faith, *and you'll find you have no care in the world!*

His provision will be your portion!

Jesus says,

'Hey come on now, not even the birds worry about tomorrow's food, or tomorrow's worms, or tomorrow's woe's even.'

Can you just imagine, and humor me now, can you imagine the worms putting out their faith,

'O, God, please don't let the birds see me today, please hide me from their sight.'

And the birds also, putting out their faith for food, putting out their faith and asking God to please allow them to catch and eat the worm today...

...but now they have a problem you see, because,

'What if God is listening to the worm's prayer today now more than mine? O, I know, maybe if I just chirp loud enough, and long enough, then God will hear me, and God will stop rescuing the worm, and maybe if I just praise my way through this problem, you know, I've got a handle on God's principles you know, all I have to do is praise long enough and loud enough and with enough put-on passion, then you know, eventually I'll overcome God's reluctance to bless me.'

And here is that little worm again, trying to be louder than the bird, and trying to get a sound in edgewise, (who knows what sounds the little worm make, ha… ha… ha… but O well, you get my point) Here is the little worm now, and he's got to try and outperform the bird and show more passion that the circumstance so God can hear him and won't overlook him today and ignore his cries.

And you see church people are no different, they think,

'Well things aren't going so good, and I still don't have my breakthrough, so maybe if I pray hard enough and intense enough and long enough and intercede enough, I can get God to do it, or maybe I can fast God into it, and if I can't fast Him into wanting to do it for me, then maybe if I give my way out of this, or if I only praise Him enough, with enough heart felt passion, maybe if I praise long enough, then maybe I can finally get my breakthrough!'

'If I praise long enough and with enough passion then I'll get there!'

Listen, what a lie, man, *it's nothing but outright ignorance on display,*

…but listen, brother, sister, *God has overlooked our times of ignorance.*

Listen *He is not mad at you man,* **He loves you!**

And listen, *He sees the desire and the sincerity of your heart that you give to Him,*

…but come on man, **discover His initiative!**

There is only one way into deep fellowship with God, *and it's the way that He opened!*

You are not going to open up another way, no way; it is not going to happen.

…not your way, His way, amen!

Do you see now how to appropriate perfect praise?

Not by something you are hoping to get, you see,

'O, if I now just praise long enough and hard enough, then He is going to give me the riches'

No,

110

…but your praise is now awakened *by something you already have!*

…it is awakened *by acknowledging every good thing that is in you,*

…that is yours already in Christ Jesus!

…every good thing *that already belongs to you, 100%.*

Stop looking at,

'O, <u>as it is</u> *we do not yet see!'*

Start looking **at Jesus!**

<u>**Look away**</u> *unto Jesus!*

Don't look at Him religiously, man, *look at Him as in a mirror!*

Hebrews 12:2,

"Looking away <u>unto Jesus</u>…"

"…the author …and finisher …of our faith!"

How do we understand Jesus?

You can only understand Him *the way God interprets Him!*

He is,

"...the author ...and the pioneer..."

Of what?

"...of MY faith!"

What is my faith?

I see my salvation,

...my redemption that is complete in Him!

And I hold on to it!

And I reject and throw out *every contradiction!*

...every other contrary opinion!

I consider it a lie *and I reject it and oppose it with my faith!*

...I deal with it effectively!

...I throw it out!

That's how we lay aside every weight, every sin!

It says in 1Corinthians 5:7, *"Cleanse yourselves from the old leaven, (from the old influence, from the old thinking) so you may be a new lump!"*

It seems an impossible task, **_how do I get rid of the old influence,_**

…of that old ignorance?

The Weiss translation says,

"*…**for in fact you are already free from the old leaven!***"

We are not just discovering **the facts,** no, *we are looking away from* **natural facts,**

…from our old way of looking of things,

…from those **natural facts,**

…even from our own failed experiences that confirmed and reinforced that old way of thinking,

…we are looking away from **those facts,**

…from that old way of thinking, from those old experiences of failure,

…**because we are discovering <u>new facts</u>,**

…facts that are of <u>greater reality</u>!

…it is a fact, I am really free, I mean it's a new fact I have discovered,

…it's a fact, <u>a reality</u>, amen!

...it's a fact, <u>a reality</u>,

...in fact <u>I am really free</u>!

...I don't need to put up with sickness or disease,

...and I don't need to try and fight it in my own strength either,

...I can rest <u>in God</u>!

...I can <u>rest</u> in my faith!

...in that <u>focus</u>!

...I can rest in my encounter with God!

...I don't need to put up with anything that would restrict my encounter of God,

...because ...in fact, I am really free!

Why?

"...because, in fact, the Passover lamb has already been slain!"

It happened, amen!

It happened *when He died!*

Hallelujah!

Thank you Father!

You are my health, amen!

You sustain my life!

You sustain me in health!

...because *In Him I was healed,*

...*and I am healed!*

...You are my healing, *and I rejoice in that!*

...I rejoice in *You,* God of my salvation!

...God who is my healer!

You are my health *and my very life!*

...*my everything!*

Amen!

Hallelujah!

Chapter 6

Let the word of Christ dwell in you richly!

In closing, go with me quickly to Colossians 3 also.

Now verse 16 says, and we quoted it already, it says,

"Let the word of Christ indwell you in rich abundance!"

The RSV says,

"Let the word of Christ dwell in you richly in all wisdom!"

What is the wisdom of God?

1Corinthians 2:7 & 8 says that,

"...it is the wisdom of God that carried the secret of man's glorification"

What God decreed concerning your glorification, *that's the wisdom of God!*

That wisdom had to be kept secret, *because God didn't want the enemy to find out His plan.*

Because he says in 1Corinthians 2:8,

"...if the enemy found out the plan of God, he would never have crucified the Lord of Glory, he would never have crucified Jesus!"

The wisdom of God *is the foolishness of the cross!*

'I mean what are we going to do with Jesus? We are going to have to get rid of Him,' the devil thought.

God in His wisdom fooled the devil, and so *the devil just contributed, towards your redemption!*

And so Paul says here in Colossians 3:16,

"Let the word of Christ indwell you richly, in rich abundance!"

What is that word of Christ?

...the wisdom of what God had in mind in Christ for man!

That wisdom, that word, *now indwells me!*

And now, *out of that rich indwelling,* I am now teaching and instructing my brothers and sisters, *in all insight and revelation.*

That word, *"revelation,"* I wrote there in the margin of my Bible, it means: **awakening one another's minds and spirits.**

You see when your mind is just there, occupied with the temporal, and your spirit also is just there, occupied with the natural, occupied with the problem, *then I want to awaken your mind and your spirit **with insight, with revelation, concerning your origin, concerning your destiny in Christ,***

…what you were created for, what you were designed for, and destined for, in Christ from the beginning!

Paul goes on to say,

*"**This will find full expression in every song you sing! Whether it is a psalm…"***

*…*and the word, *"**psalm**"* means **to rave about God in praise, accompanied by musical instruments!**

How do you rave about God?

'Draw me nearer, nearer, nearer Lord to thee…'

No,

Ha... ha... ha...

Hallelujah!

The word, *"halal"* means **to rave, to get exceedingly crazy about something!**

But you see I'm not just going to get that by just letting my mind and spirit wonder around,

...no, it's the rich indwelling of the word!

The more I draw upon, the more I draw from what God reveals in Jesus, from what God spoke to me in His son, Jesus Christ, and every prophet confirms it, even the law confirms it, all that God spoke in the old covenant writings points towards it, and I see my total release there in Him, and I am drawing from it, and I draw from it, and in my fellowship of the saints also, I am communicating every good thing that is in us in Christ Jesus, and what happens?

A song is born, and I grab an instrument, perhaps a guitar, or another instrument, and a couple of my friends **and I begin to *RAVE* about the greatness of God!**

*...*and suddenly my *rave* has another volume, *because it has another source of information,*

...it's no longer trying to get to God as if He is far away,

120

...it is no longer trying to get nearer to God,

...and it is no longer trying to measure God with all the silver and gold and all the nice things the world see as valuable,

...but it is God's very own salvation expressed in it,

...expressed in my rave!

...volumes upon volumes of it,

...volumes upon volumes of God's truth and love, overwhelming my soul, filling me with glee and delight!

...and I rave about the goodness of God!

...and I rave about God and who He is!

...and I rave about who He is to me!

...and about His love for me!

...and I express my love and appreciation and excitement and enjoyment back to Him!

You see Deity has found His home in the heart of man again!

Alright now, Paul says,

"This will find full expression in every song you sing! Whether it is a psalm..."

"...or a hymn..."

A hymn is a testimony song.

"...or a song in the spirit..."

A new, spontaneous song

The revelation of Grace (what God accomplished in Christ on our behalf) will inspire your hearts to minister to God in song!

You see there is only one source now *that inspires your praise!*

It's the revelation of grace!

My life has found a new definition in grace, in redemption!

Amen!

I am what I am, *by the grace of God!*

And His grace towards me was not in vain!

You see grace comes to reign, and it causes me, through the gift of righteousness, to rule, in life,

...having all things subject to you!

God doesn't have anything else in mind for you!

'O, you know, brother, it is a long process of renewing your mind.'

'...and while I have only 20% of my mind renewed the devil will still have all the access he needs for many, many years, until I finally have it like 80% renewed or so'

Ha... ha... ha...

No, nonsense man!

How long does it take to renew your mind?

Only as long as it takes to grasp and embrace the revelation!

...and after that, your problem is no longer the renewing of the mind, *but the appropriation, the practical application of the word!*

Most Christian's problem is not the renewing of the mind, but they have a problem *because they fail to apply the word!*

That's it, that's their problem, it's not complicated, it's that simple!

They can no longer blame the devil, or the renewing of the mind, or whatever else,

...whatever process they want to attach their distance and delay mentality to.

They have no one to blame but themselves!

Their problem is, *they fail to apply the word practically to their thinking and to their lives!*

That's it!

Okay let's just quickly finish up there in Colossians,

"Let the word of Christ richly dwell within you..."

Now Chapter 3:1 says,

"Since you are in fact co-raised with Christ,"

Is that in fact what God says to you in Christ?

Yes, He does say that, amen!

He says, *you are co-raised with Christ!*

Now let that, *richly indwell* you!

In all wisdom!

That means, apply it to your life!

It means, don't be ignorant any longer concerning the fact that you have been co-raised with Jesus!

None of your own works will at all co-raise you, amen!

You are as co-raised as can be, amen!

You are as dead as can be!

You are as dead to sin as can be!

In Jesus you died, amen!

If Jesus died you died!

There in Him you died to the power of sin!

You died!

You are as dead as can be, amen!

There is no process, no future event that is going to add to that!

You died in Him, amen!

The whole of Colossians 2 speaks of that.

And now Colossians 3:1 says,

"If then in fact you are co-raised with Jesus,"

Wow what a logical and powerful conclusion to the gospel!

How do I appropriate that!

It is now logical; it is only obvious that your focus must now be upon the things that are above!

...things that relate to this position of being co-raised and co-seated with Christ!

He says,

"Since then in fact you are co-raised with Jesus, set your mind on the things that are above, where Christ is seated at the right hand of God!"

...and you see, "If then in fact you were co-raised with Him,"

...then Paul comes to the right conclusion, to the only conclusion one can possibly come to and he says back there, in Ephesians 2:6 that,

"...you are co-seated with Christ in heaven (in that realm of spirit reality!),"

...and also here in verse 3,

"...for you died, and your life is now hidden with Christ in God!"

Verse 2 says,

"Concentrate your mind upon these things, rather than to be occupied with earthly things"

To be, *"occupied"* with earthly things means **to praise earthly things,**

...or to price and value and treasure earthly things!

He says,

Verse 3,

"You already died in His death. The secret of your life now is your union with Christ in God!"

"Every time Christ is revealed as being our life, (either to us in the Scriptures, or out of us, because of our living faith; because we are living by that faith,)

"Every time Christ is revealed as being our life, then we are being co-revealed in the same glory, being united together with Him!"

And now this is how he ends off in verse 5, he says,

"Consider..."

So, this is now how you put away every weight and the sin which ensnares you,

...this is how you put off every sin so close at hand, the sin which clings to you,

...this is now how you get cleansed in your very conduct,

"Consider the members of your earthly body as dead!"

...as dead, amen!

"Consider it as dead. Consider the members of your earthly body as dead towards fornication (sexual uncleanness), lusts (unhealthy passions or inappropriate desires) and covetousness, which is just another form of idol worship."

In verse 7 he says,

"You used to live this way; your life and members subject to the dominion of Sin and of sins,"

"But now..."

Verse 8,

"But now you can permanently rid yourselves of all these things. Things such as wrath (a bad temper), malice (harboring ill feelings in your heart towards another person, and plotting evil against them), slander (saying negative ugly things against someone else behind their back, even untrue things, bad mouthing them in public to other people, this include any attempts to belittle someone else, and to cause them to fall into disrepute, or to receive a bad reputation – the Greek word

there is the word commonly used for blasphemy),"

*"...**you can also rid yourself of such things as envy (jealousy, coveting someone else's goods, or their life or their wife, and coming against them because of those things in your heart, even going so far as trying to get those things from them and making it your own) and (you can thus permanently rid yourself of) every form of irregular behavior or irregular language.***"*

He says in verse 9,

*"**Hey listen, you don't need to give a false impression to one another or to any other person, seeing that the old man together with its practices have been utterly stripped of its authority in your life, and you have clothed yourself with the new creation,***"*

Verse 10 says,

*"...**and therefore now, you are renewed in the exact knowledge of your Creator, according to the design and image of your Creator.***"*

...and verse 11,

*"**It is no longer important what you were by natural birth, whether you were a Greek or a Jew, circumcised or uncircumcised. Listen,***

what matters now is the fact that Christ is in you! You are the product of God's love"

Do you see that?

Immediately, when I discover God's approval of my life, *I find a new volume of appreciation,*

…I find a new volume even in my appreciation of my brother and sister, *and of my fellow man.*

…I put off from me; I get rid of…

Just recently when I got into Atlanta after a long flight I met an old friend at the airport and he had lost quite a considerable amount of weight, and so I couldn't help but comment the moment I saw him, *'Wow brother, you lost a lot of weight since I last saw you,'* and in his usual crass manner he said to me, *'**I didn't lose it, I got rid of it!**'*

Ha… ha… ha…

That made me laugh, it was just what I needed to refresh my spirits.

I thought to myself,

*'Hallelujah, he didn't lose it, **he got rid of it,** otherwise, if he lost it he can find it again, but seeing that he got rid of it **it's not coming back!**'*

Ha… ha… ha…

130

Amen, when it comes to sin, get rid of it, and don't pick it back up again as if you just temporarily lost it or shook it off, but now it's back!

No, man, **get rid of it!**

Ha… ha… ha…

The word says,

"You can rid yourself, permanently, from a bad temper, from irregular language, and irregular behavior that you are taking out on other people and hurting them with in any way."

How did you do it?

By setting your eyes on the things that are above!

What's above?

You are co-raised and co-seated with Christ Jesus **in a place of authority over these things, not just above, far above, all rule and principality and power and might and dominion of the enemy, amen!**

You are co-raised and co-seated with Christ Jesus!

Occupy your mind with that!

Don't let your mind be distracted into earthly things, into someone else's opinion that contradicts and tries to undo God's opinion, amen!

Hallelujah!

God's opinion is permanent!

…and now His opinion rules me, in my meditation, in my conversation, and in my attitude, and in my actions, my whole behavior, my whole conduct!

You see my whole conduct becomes my worship,

…it becomes the visible testimony of where my faith is plugged into.

Really you see, it is just a matter of making up your mind **with your heart,**

…making up your mind about His provision concerning your liberty and victory in Christ!

You see, **your mouth will talk** *where your heart is plugged into!*

If your heart is plugged into your problem, then, oh brother, you'll discover the detail of it, and more and more information about it that will justify your misery,

...and that problem becomes more and more powerful until it totally overwhelms you!

But hey, listen; *plug your heart into the things that are above!*

...come into exclusive fellowship with the revelation of Christ!

"Let the word of Christ dwell in you richly"

Do you know where the faith necessary to overcome your problem comes from?

Do you know where faith comes from?

Romans 10:17 says that that faith **comes from the word of Christ,** *from the revelation of Christ!*

"So, then, faith comes by hearing, and hearing by the word of Christ!"

I know some translations say,

"...by the word of God"

But that sounds like law again. It actually says there,

"...the word of Christ!"

"So, then, faith comes by hearing, and hearing by the word of Christ (by the revelation of Christ)!"

What God said in Christ, *that's what gives faith,* amen!

That's where our faith comes from!

From what God said in Christ!

You can read the law all day long, *but you don't get faith by reading the law.*

You can read the Scriptures all day long, *but you don't get faith by just reading the Scriptures either.*

You get faith from reading and understanding Christ; *what God has to say to us in Christ, what God has to say to you in Jesus,*

...the word of His power that upholds the universe!

***Hey that word alone is power* and it upholds the universe!**

Listen God is so totally involved and so totally committed to what he has said about you in Jesus!

He sees the whole universe only in the light of that.

God doesn't see any reason for the universe to be there, outside of His plan with you!

Hallelujah!

Listen, pondering and musing on God's appreciation of you *will fuel your appreciation of Him.*

And so, the only way that you could perfectly praise Him, *is by perfectly appropriating what He has made possible for you to enjoy!*

...frequenting Him daily in your closet, frequenting Him, visiting with Him in the private place, communing with Him in the privacy of your heart!

...frequent Him in your conversation also.

In the book of Job we read how Job's devotion became so restricted to a religious ritual, to just daily doing his morning devotions, daily just quickly offering up burnt offerings, you know, *just for in case someone sinned you know, then at least he would be covered,*

...and he became so sin-conscious that it totally dominated his whole relationship with God,

…and something inevitably died in his relationship with God and got replaced by mere ritual.

Sin-consciousness totally dominated his conversation with God, and I'm sure with others also, and it dictated his whole life; *his whole life began to revolve around it.*

He was in bondage and didn't even know it!

He turned what used to be a beautiful relationship and friendship with God into law; into something that is totally dominated and dictated to by the law!

He did that, God didn't do that to their relationship. Job did that all by himself!

…and so we also read there how Satan came and challenged the quality of Job's relationship with God, and said to God,

'God, do you know why Job is so righteous, it's because you set a hedge around him. How would you even know that what you have with Job in relationship is real? I bet if he loses everything, he will end up cursing you, and not be quite so righteous anymore. Job only loves you because of what he can get from you! It is obvious to me that he is relying on his works to uphold this relationship with you, he doesn't really trust You, or love You, God, it's all fake, he only does what he does so You can keep

protecting his stuff. He loves his stuff more than You!'

...and we know the rest of the story, how Job's relationship with God was tested by the enemy who wanted to embarrass God and destroy Job in the process,

...and how the enemy succeeded in making Job lose faith in God, and basically in self-righteousness begin to accuse God of unrighteousness, just like the enemy predicted he would!

Satan proved once again that he had the human race firmly in his grip through the Fall!

But, ha... ha... ha... his celebration was short lived, because God took Job into a much deeper relationship with Him, through revelation knowledge,

...and God brought him to a place in faith, to where that intimacy and relationship could no longer be challenged by circumstances!

You see God had to introduce to Job a new platform of fellowship called, *righteousness by faith,*

...based on Job's discovery of <u>God's initiative</u> in their relationship, *because God didn't want Job distracted ever again in their relationship!*

God doesn't want you distracted from righteousness by faith, through any teaching that contradicts it!

Don't allow any teaching to distract you from intimacy with Him!

Don't try and believe God for breakthroughs in your life anymore man, *just fix your gaze,*

...just concentrate your faith now on fellowshipping in His favor,

...just enjoy His favor,

...just enjoy that favor He has already given you so abundantly!

...and in the enjoyment of that favor you'll soon begin to discover His voice,

...as you get wrapped up in that favor, *as you get caught up in His favor,*

...he says, *"Do you not know that you are of much more value than the birds ...than many birds!"*

"...Do not be anxious therefore, My beloved, but rest in what you see, BELIEVE, trust, and be persuaded in what you see in My love,

...in that favor you see there in My love,

...for it is real and trustworthy and reliable."

"...Don't you know, My favor is upon you! It is as reliable as I am reliable! I am reliable in my love! Just trust in Me, rest in that, keep focusing upon that! Keep focusing on what you have seen, on what I have shown you in redemption, in My Son, and do not become distracted by anything that tries to speak and say anything contrary to that,

...contrary to what I have already said to you and confirmed in My Son!"

Listen man, you don't have to try and get anywhere with God, *you are there already!*

Faith enters into His rest!

Nowhere in the New Testament, that's now after His resurrection okay, nowhere in any of the writings of the apostles does it ever tell us to, or try to encourage us again, *to be hungry for God.*

You can try and go hunt for it, but you won't find those scriptures there, on the contrary, we're told by the apostles that our union with Christ eradicates hunger from our lives forever!

That fellowship we enjoy in His bosom, that faith based fellowship we enjoy on a daily basis eradicates hunger forever and replaces it with fullness!

Of His fullness have we all received!

...and we are complete in Him!

Our lives are now hidden with Christ in God!

We are now seated with Him in heavenly places!

That's where we are, that's where we *live!*

In a place of fullness and contentment!

We have entered His rest, wrapped up in His bosom!

Dwelling constantly, daily in His presence, in a place of abiding with Him!

In Your presence Lord, there is fullness of Joy!

...and at Your right hand there are pleasures forevermore!

Hallelujah! Praise You Jesus!

Thank you Father God!

Looking for a way to impact the world through our praise and worship, and seeking to be relevant often makes us become irrelevant.

But if we can simply learn to abide in that place of fullness and include the world in it, and reveal to them, even in our songs, *how included they already are,* we immediately and automatically become relevant, totally totally relevant!

...ministering from heaven itself, ministering from out of His presence, *imparting His nearness, imparting His very presence!*

How much more relevant than that do you want to get?

You can't get any more relevant than that!

Encounter with God, *experiencing His nearness,* is what it's all about!

That is as relevant as relevant can be!

Only singing and ministering and living *from this place of faith,* can bring that about permanently!

And let me tell you something, that faith is so much more than a choice, so much more than a decision.

Faith is a discovery!

The love of God realized awakens that belief!

Faith is not blind, neither is it unconscious; faith KNOWS!

Faith is a place of persuasion!

Faith is a conviction in the truth!

...a total persuasion in what God has revealed and already made possible for you to enjoy!

Faith is the place of living in the victory 24/7!

Faith is the place of meeting!

Faith is the place of encounter!

Faith is the place of rest!

Faith is the place of fulfillment!

Faith is a place of fullness!

If my effectiveness in ministry or in my Christian life has to do with the price I'm willing to pay, *to try and produce it,* then my friend, I may want to seriously reconsider even buying the product!

Listen, Jesus already paid it all, *so I can enjoy the fullness of God and live in the fullness and minister out of that place of fullness!*

Listen, you who are a citizen of the USA, like I am, **you already are one; *you don't have to try and become one!***

…you don't have to try and become what you already are!

…and you don't have to try and get into a place where you already are, **you are already there!**

Separate yourself from everything seeking to convince you that you're again separated in some way from God,

…and separate yourself unto that which speaks of your union with Him!

Just enjoy, just appreciate and enjoy, *what He has already made possible for you to enjoy!*

In closing, I urge you to get yourself a copy of *"The Mirror Bible"* available online at: www.friendsofthemirror.com or at www.amazon.com and several other book sellers.

If you want me or someone a part of our team to come to where you are, anywhere in the world, and give a talk or teach you and some of your friends about the gospel message, and this magnificent work of redemption, simply contact us at www.livingwordintl.com …or you can always find me on www.facebook.com

If you have been helped, or your perspective on life has changed, as a result of reading this book, please get in touch with me and let me know.

I would love to share your joy,

…so that my joy in writing this book may be full!

"For this reason I bow my knees
to the Father of our Lord Jesus
Christ,

from whom the whole family
in Heaven and earth **is named,**

that He would grant you,

according to the riches of His
glory,

to be strengthened with might
through His Spirit
in your inner man,

(His Spirit uses His Word to do
this)

that Christ may dwell in your
hearts through faith;
that you may be rooted
and grounded
in Love,

and may be able to comprehend
together with all the saints

the width, length , depth, and
height of it - to intimately know
the love of Christ

which far surpasses mere knowledge;

so that you may be filled with all the fullness of God"

~ Ephesians 3:14-19

"That which was from the beginning,
...which we have heard
(not just with our ears,
but with our spiritual ears),
...which we have also seen
(not just with our eyes,
but with our spiritual eyes)
...which we have looked upon
(...gazed at, beheld,
focused our attention upon),

...and which our hands have also
handled

(...which we have also
experienced,
not just in the physical realm,
but in our inner man),

...concerning the Word of life,

...we declare (make known) to
you,

...that you also may have this
fellowship with us;

...for truly our fellowship
is with the Father,

and with His Son,
Jesus Christ.

*And **these things we write to you
that your joy may be full.***"

1 John 1:1-4

About The Author

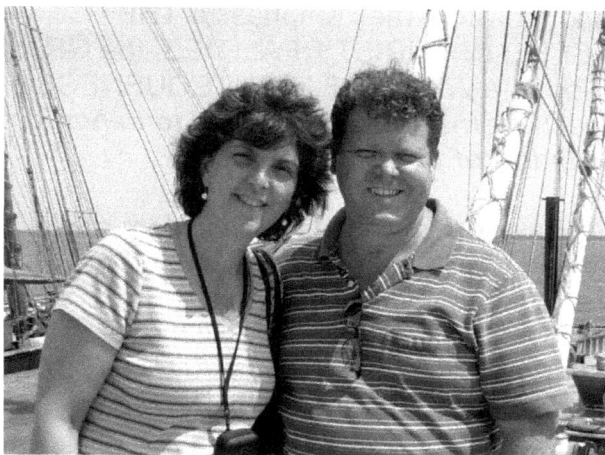

Rudi & Carmen Louw together oversee and pastor a church: Living Word International.

Rudi was born and raised in the country of South Africa while Carmen grew up in Cortland, New York. Today they travel and minister both locally and internationally.

They function in the ministry of reconciliation (2Corinthians 5:18-21) and flow strongly in the gifts of the Holy Spirit and His anointing to teach, preach, prophecy, heal *and whatever is needed to touch people's lives with the reality of God's love and power.*

God has given them keen insight into what He has to say to mankind in the work of redemption, *concerning the revelation of, and restoration of,* **humanity's true identity,**

...and therefore they emphasize THE GOSPEL; IN CHRIST REALITIES; the GRACE of God; the WORD OF RIGHTEOUSNESS *and all such eternal truths* **essential to salvation and living of the CHRIST-LIFE**

They have been granted this wisdom and revelation into the knowledge of God by the Spirit of Truth; by the resurrected Spirit of Jesus Christ Himself, *to establish and strengthen believers* **in THE FAITH OF GOD, and to activate them in ministering to others.**

Not only are people set free from the poison and bondage of sin, condemnation and all kinds of intimidation, (upheld, strengthened and reinforced by age old religious ideas born out of ignorance and deception,) *but many are brought into a closer more intimate relationship with Father God,* **as Daddy,** *through accurate teaching, and unveiling of the gospel message, prophetic words, healings and miracles.*

Rudi & Carmen are closely knitted together with many other effective Christians, church fellowships, and groups of believers *who share the same revelation and passion* **to impart God's TRUTH; to make disciples, and to impact the world with the LOVE OF GOD.**

www.ingramcontent.com/pod-product-compliance
Lightning Source LLC
Chambersburg PA
CBHW051843090426
42736CB00011B/1931